Building
Squishy Circuits

By AnnMarie Thomas, Kristin Fontichiaro, and Sage Thomas

Published in the United States of America by
Cherry Lake Publishing
Ann Arbor, Michigan
www.cherrylakepublishing.com

Series Editor: Kristin Fontichiaro
Photo Credits: Cover and page 14, Kristin Fontichiaro;
    pages 4 and 18, Michigan Makers/University of Michigan;
    pages 6, 8, 10, 12, and 16, AnnMarie and Sage Thomas;
    page 20, Pamela Williams

Library of Congress Cataloging-in-Publication Data
Names: Thomas, AnnMarie P., author. | Fontichiaro, Kristin, author. | Thomas, Sage,
    author.
Title: Building squishy circuits / by AnnMarie Thomas, Kristin Fontichiaro, and Sage
    Thomas.
Description: Ann Arbor, Michigan : Cherry Lake Publishing, [2018] | Series: Makers as
    innovators junior | Audience: Grade K to grade 3. | Includes bibliographical references
    and index.
Identifiers: LCCN 2017000102| ISBN 9781634726900 (lib. bdg.) | ISBN 9781634727563
    (pdf) | ISBN 9781634727235 (pbk.) | ISBN 9781634727891 (ebook)
Subjects: LCSH: Electronic circuit design—Technique—Juvenile literature. | Polymer clay
    craft—Juvenile literature. | Play-Doh (Toy)—Juvenile literature.
Classification: LCC TK7820 .T47 2018 | DDC 621.3815—dc23 LC record available at
    https://lccn.loc.gov/2017000102

Cherry Lake Publishing would like to acknowledge the work of the Partnership for
21st Century Learning. Please visit *www.p21.org* for more information.

Printed in the United States of America
Corporate Graphics

Note: Squishy Circuits® is a registered trademark of Squishy Circuits Store, LLC, and is
used with permission.

A Note to Adults: Please review the instructions for the activities in this book before allowing children to do them. Be sure to help them with any activities you do not think they can safely complete on their own.

A Note to Kids: Be sure to ask an adult for help with these activities when you need it. Always put your safety first!

Table of Contents

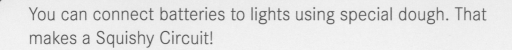

You can connect batteries to lights using special dough. That makes a Squishy Circuit!

What Are Squishy Circuits?

Electricity is all around us. It lights our houses, powers our phones, and makes our toys work. Whenever you plug something in or add batteries, you are using electricity. Electricity flows in a circular path called a **circuit**. Squishy Circuits are a fun way to build circuits at home. You can use dough to connect the parts of the circuit together.

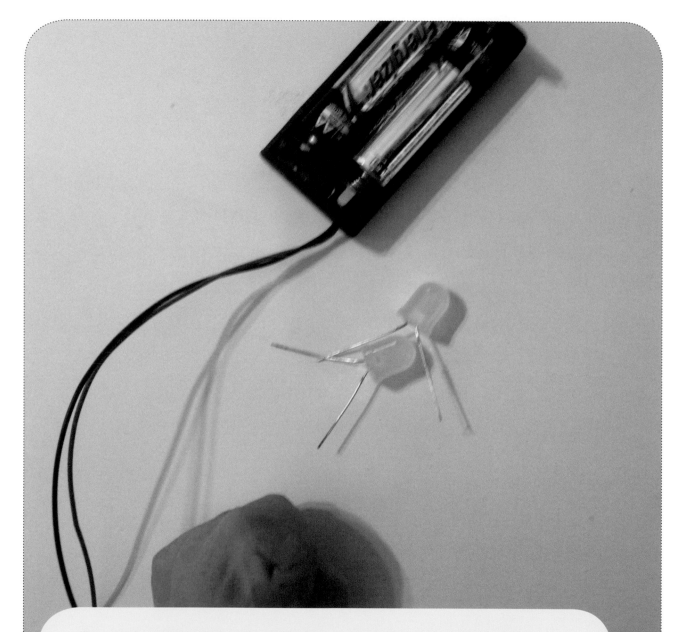

The main things you will need are a battery pack with 2 AA batteries, LED bulbs, and dough.

Supplies

To build Squishy Circuits, you will need:

- 2-AA battery pack with wires
- Two AA batteries
- At least five 10-mm **LED** bulbs
- Activity dough (store-bought or homemade—recipe at *http:// squishycircuits.com*)

Be Safe!

Practice good circuit design safety. Do not touch the wires to each other. Do not connect LEDs directly to the wires, either.

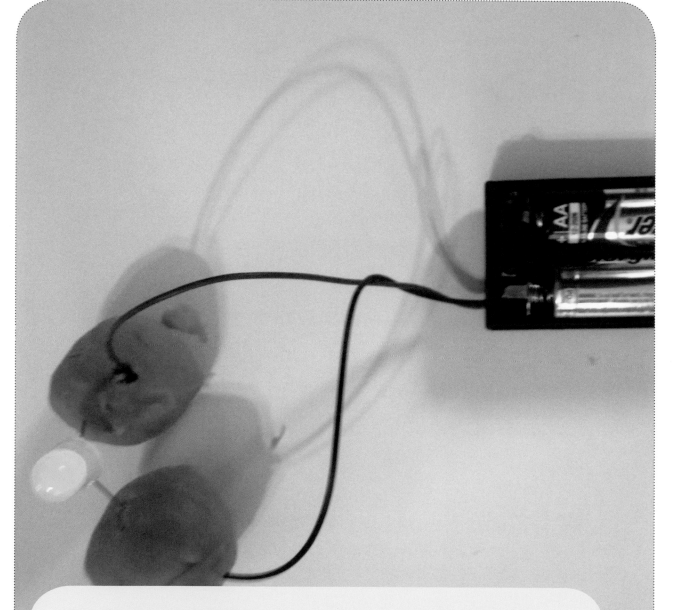

This Squishy Circuit works! If yours does not, check the battery pack switch or the LED legs.

Making Your First Circuit

Start by rolling two balls of dough. Push one wire from the battery pack into each of the balls. Make sure the balls are not touching each other. Now put one of the LED's legs into each of the balls. Turn on the battery pack if it has a switch. If your LED does not light up, switch the LED legs going into the dough balls.

Why Does Switching LED Legs Matter?

LEDs only allow electricity to flow in one direction. If they are put into the circuit backward, they will block the electricity. The LED will not light up. Your LED probably has one leg that is a little longer than the other. This leg goes into the dough with the red wire.

Electricity likes to move in a closed loop. Can you see where the loop is open here? How would you fix it?

What's Happening in Your Circuit?

Electricity will only flow if the circuit forms a complete loop. In this circuit, the electricity flows from the battery pack into the first dough ball. Then it goes through the LED to the second dough ball. Finally, it goes back into the battery pack. If you unplug the battery pack from the dough, the loop is incomplete. The LED will not light up.

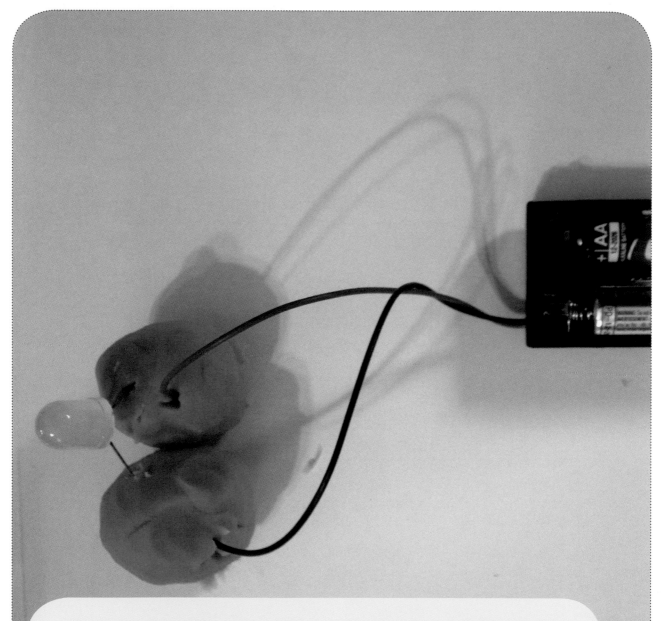

The balls of dough are touching each other. This is a short circuit. The LED does not turn on.

Short Circuits

Test your circuit to see what happens when you push the two balls of dough together. Did your LED turn off? That happened because allowing the two balls to touch is causing a **short circuit**. The electricity skips the LED. Separate the two balls of dough so that they are no longer touching. This should make the LED light up again.

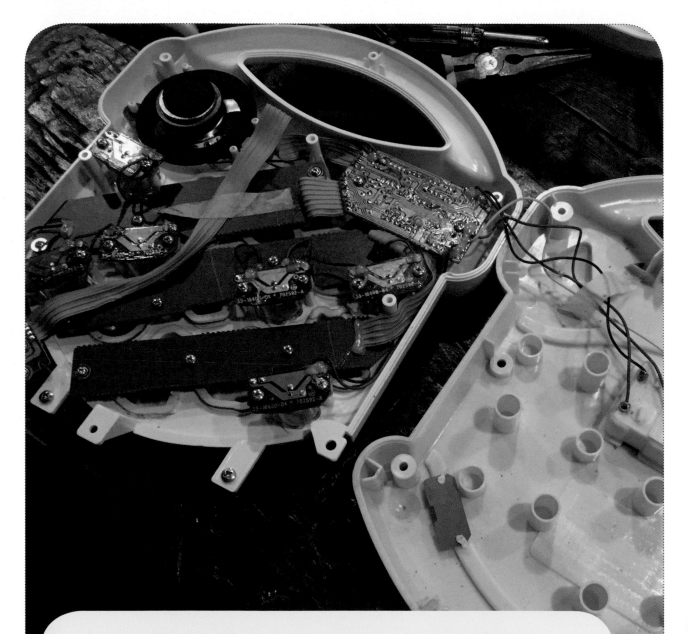

It is easy to spot a short circuit in a simple electrical device. Finding a short circuit inside a complex toy like this one can be trickier!

What Happens in a Short Circuit?

In your short circuit, the electricity flowed through the touching balls of dough and back into the battery pack. It skipped the LED. This is because the dough path is easier for the electricity to go through.

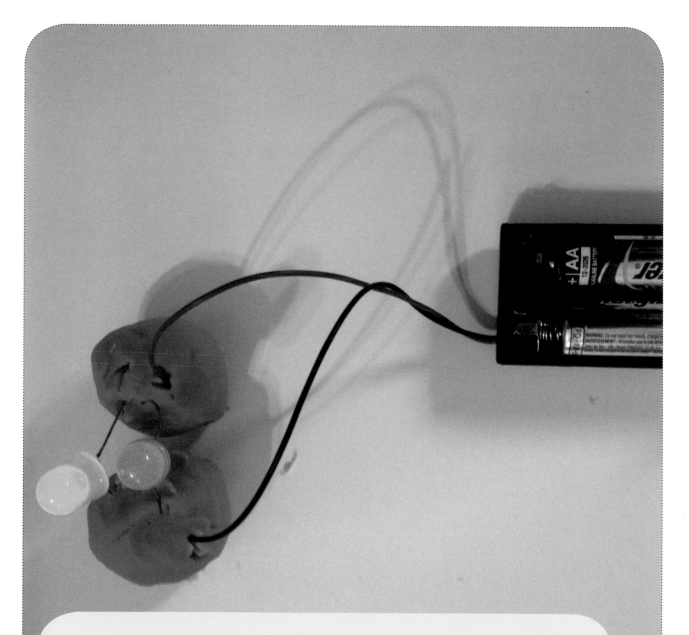

In this parallel circuit, the electricity flows from the battery pack's black wire to the dough. It then completes two paths: one for the blue LED and another for the green LED.

Adding More Lights: Parallel Circuits

Let's add another light to your circuit. Simply attach another LED to the balls of dough. Does it light up right away? If not, try switching the legs that go into each ball of dough. As the electricity flows, the circuit's path splits to go through both LEDs. This is called a **parallel circuit**.

This student used a bigger battery pack. This means she had more electricity to power her parallel circuits. How many lights can you add?

How Many Lights Can You Add?

You might notice that your LEDs get dimmer as you add more bulbs. The battery splits its energy among all of the LEDs you use. When the bulbs need more energy than the batteries have, they can only light up a little bit. When that happens, try taking an LED away. Do the others get brighter?

Clean Up!

Always remove the batteries from your battery pack when you are done using it. Wipe down the LEDs after you use them. The salt in the dough can **corrode** the legs if you do not wipe them down.

Try building a paper circuit using copper tape and other supplies.

What Can You Do Next?

Now that you have made some circuits, try other kinds of electrical projects. You might take toys apart and see what their circuits look like inside. You could play with toys like Snap Circuits or littleBits. You could make **paper circuits**. You could help adults fix broken things. There is so much you can do when you use electricity safely!

Glossary

circuit (SUR-kit) a closed loop for electricity to travel through

corrode (kuh-ROHD) to destroy or eat away at something

LED (EL EE DEE) a small bulb that lights up when electricity passes through it; **LED** stands for "light-emitting diode"

paper circuits (PAY-pur SUR-kits) circuits built on paper using batteries, copper tape, and other supplies

parallel circuit (PAR-uh-lel SUR-kit) a circuit where the electricity splits into two or more paths and then reconnects

short circuit (SHORT SUR-kit) a mistake in your circuit, when electricity does not go where you want it to

Find Out More

Books

Fontichiaro, Kristin. *Taking Toys Apart*. Ann Arbor, MI: Cherry Lake Publishing, 2018.

Fontichiaro, Kristin, and AnnMarie P. Thomas. *Squishy Circuits*. Ann Arbor, MI: Cherry Lake Publishing, 2015.

Williams, Pamela. *Paper Circuits*. Ann Arbor, MI: Cherry Lake Publishing, 2018.

Web Sites

DK Find Out!—Circuits
www.dkfindout.com/us/science/electricity/circuits
Learn more about different types of circuits.

Squishy Circuits
http://squishycircuits.com
Learn more about Squishy Circuits and order supplies.

Index

About the Authors

AnnMarie Thomas is an engineering professor at the University of St. Thomas. Kristin Fontichiaro teaches and makes things at the University of Michigan School of Information. Sage Thomas is an elementary school student in St. Paul, Minnesota.